Ventures In Thinking
TEACHER SERIES

P9-EMC-564

Graphic Templates for Structured Thinking Skills

VOLUME 1

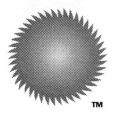

Ventures In Thinking
TEACHER SERIES

Graphic Templates for
Structured Thinking Skills

VOLUME 1

VENTURES EDUCATION SYSTEMS CORPORATION

Ventures In Thinking
TEACHER SERIES

Graphic Templates for Structured Thinking Skills
Volume 1

Copyright © 2003 Ventures Education Systems Corporation.

All rights reserved. No part of this publication may be reproduced or transmitted in any form or by any means, electronic or mechanical, including photocopying, recording, or any information storage and retrieval means, without permission from the copyright holder.

ISBN 0-9716903-1-6

Printed in the United States of America.
10 9 8 7 6 5 4 3 2 1

Cover design and illustrations: Alexandra Leff

VENTURES EDUCATION SYSTEMS CORPORATION
15 Maiden Lane • Suite 200 • New York, NY 10038 USA
Telephone: 212-566-2522 or 800-947-6278 • Fax: 212-566-2536
Web site: http://www.vesc-education.com
E-mail: info@ventures.org

This volume has been a collaborative effort by the editorial staff of Ventures Education Systems Corporation. The following people are acknowledged for their originality and creativity:

Editor-in-Chief
Thomas Trocco

Writers
Lorraine Janet Dean
Judith Gudgen

Graphic Template Designers
Sandra Parks
Thomas Trocco

Production Editor
Barbara Beard

Graphic Designer
Alexandra Leff

Contents

This book contains a series of Graphic Templates that can be used with the Structured Thinking Skills that are introduced in the Ventures In Thinking Teacher Series volume, *Constructive Communication and Structured Thinking in the Classroom, Volume 1.*

This book includes the Graphic Templates and Charts outlining the mental steps for the following Structured Thinking Skills:

- Defining
- Describing
- Examining Similarities and Differences
- Analyzing the Parts of a Whole
- Categorizing
- Grouping
- Ordering by Time
- Ordering by Rank
- Ordering by Occurrence
- Supporting a Conclusion

OVERVIEW

Graphic Templates provide students with a visual way to lay out facts and how they are related. When students are first learning the mental steps of a Structured Thinking Skill, they should have a copy of the Graphic Template to write on or use as a reference. When students have worked with a Graphic Template a number of times they will be able to create their own. This should be encouraged, ensuring all the mental steps are incorporated. Students will then better understand that Graphic Templates are visual representations of the mental steps that we go through when performing a thinking skill.

Without understanding the purpose of Graphic Templates, students will see them as just another worksheet with blanks to fill in. When students view Graphic Templates as tools for the expression of their thinking, they will not be limited by their format. We do not want students to stop thinking during a step of a skill simply because they run out of room, or waste time searching for something to write simply because there is room for more information. Remember we want to push the thinking and learning as far as possible.

CLASSROOM PRACTICE

Give students easy access to the Graphic Templates as reference tools. Place a copy in their work files or portfolios or post larger versions on the walls.

The first few times that you teach a skill, model how the thinking is laid out on the chalkboard, on chart paper, or on a large, poster-sized version of the Graphic Template. You will find that students quickly learn how to lay out their thinking and will not need the template in front of them.

Once students are familiar with the steps in a particular skill, they should create their own version of the Graphic Template rather than fill in a blank photocopy. They might create one in their notebooks, if working individually, or on chart paper at their table, if they are working in teams.

Students need to organize the information in a way that is meaningful to them. They may use boxes, a web layout, a branching diagram, or a design that speaks to them and catches their imagination. For example, one student or team might decide to draw branches on a tree using Analyzing the Parts of a Whole to examine an ecosystem. The important thing is that they verbalize their thinking as they are doing the mental processing.

Each student's or team's Graphic Template may look different. This does not matter as long as they have gone through the mental steps. Have students share with their classmates and explain how they have graphically organized the information. You can post responses on the classroom walls. Students will see that there are different forms that they can use and will become skilled at using the one that best suits their needs and imagination. Remember that it is the mental steps that are important, not the representation.

STUDENT GUIDE TO GRAPHIC TEMPLATES

- Graphic Templates are a way to lay out facts

- Graphic Templates demonstrate the relationships between facts in a visual way

- The Graphic Template and charts containing the steps are useful props when learning the skill

- Make the Graphic Template work for you: Don't be limited by space or the number of boxes

- As soon as you know the steps, begin to create your own Graphic Templates

Copyright © Ventures Education Systems Corporation 2003

USING OR CREATING A GRAPHIC TEMPLATE FOR DEFINING

For directions on teaching Defining and ideas for learning activities, reference Chapter 6 in the Ventures In Thinking Teacher Series volume, *Constructive Communication and Structured Thinking in the Classroom, Volume 1.*

Students should have access to the Graphic Template as a reference, for example, a copy placed in their file or posted on the wall. Once they are familiar with the steps in the skill they should create their own Graphic Template in their notebooks, rather than fill in a blank photocopy.

The first few times that you teach the skill, model how it is laid out on a chalkboard or chart. You will find that students quickly learn how to lay out the skills and will not need a template in front of them.

- In the center of the page, write the name of the person, place, thing, or idea that you are defining.

- Underneath this, identify the large category to which it belongs.

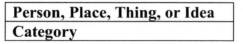

| **Person, Place, Thing, or Idea** |
| **Category** |

- Branching off of this, state the defining attributes and detail that set this person place, thing, or idea apart from all the other members of the group.

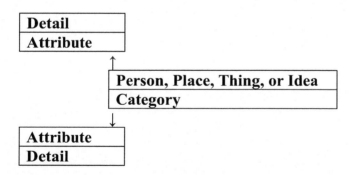

- Once students decide that they have identified enough attributes to set the person, place, thing, or idea apart from all other members of the group, ask them to write a definition at the bottom of the page.

Definition

Students may want to make changes to the information as they articulate their thinking or listen to the ideas of other members of the group. Ensure that you allow them time to modify and refine the information on their Graphic Template.

DEFINING

Step One*:* Name the large group to which the item belongs.

Step Two: Give enough attributes to set the item apart from every other member of the group. Ask, "Have I identified enough attributes to set it apart?" "Do other members share these attributes?" If they do, state more.

Step Three: Now state a definition, for example, "A _____ is_____."

DEFINING

Step One: Name the large category to which the item belongs.

Step Two: State enough defining attributes to set the item apart from every other member of the category.

Use this question as a check: "Have I identified enough attributes to set it apart from all other members of the group?" If not, state more attributes.

Step Three: State a definition.

Copyright © Ventures Education Systems Corporation 2003

DEFINING

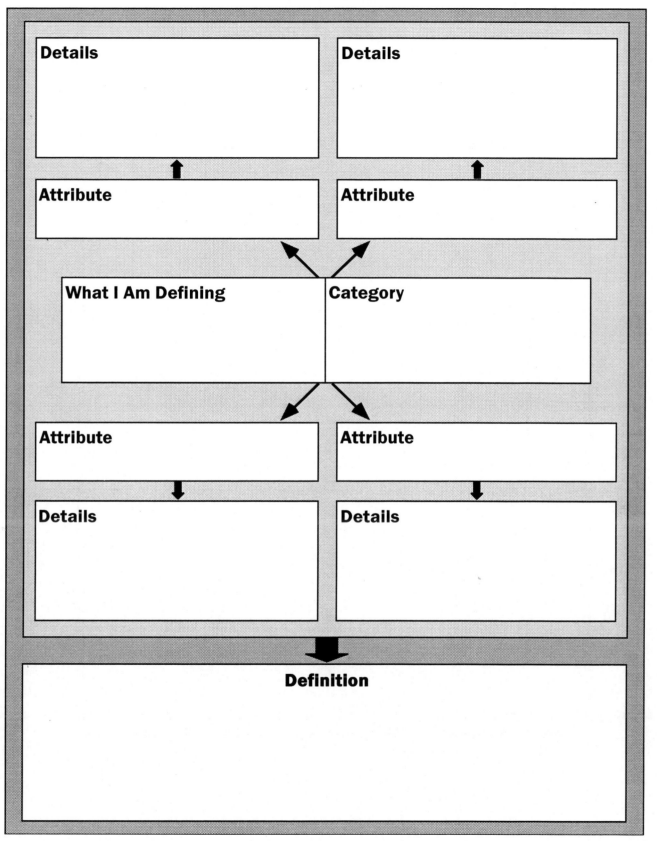

Details	Details

Attribute	Attribute

What I Am Defining	Category

Attribute	Attribute

Details	Details

Definition

Copyright © Ventures Education Systems Corporation 2003

DEFINING

Step One: Name the large group to which the item belongs.

Step Two: Give enough attributes to set the item apart from every other member of the group. Ask, "Have I identified enough attributes to set it apart?" "Do other members share these attributes?" If they do, state more.

Step Three: Now state a definition, for example, "A _____ is_____."

Copyright © Ventures Education Systems Corporation 2003

DEFINING

Step One: Name the large category to which the item belongs.

Step Two: State enough defining attributes to set the item apart from every other member of the category.

Use this question as a check: "Have I identified enough attributes to set it apart from all other members of the group?" If not, state more attributes.

Step Three: State a definition.

Copyright © Ventures Education Systems Corporation 2003

USING OR CREATING A GRAPHIC TEMPLATE FOR DESCRIBING

For directions on teaching Describing and ideas for learning activities, reference Chapter 7 in the Ventures In Thinking Teacher Series volume, *Constructive Communication and Structured Thinking in the Classroom, Volume 1.*

Students should have access to the Graphic Template as a reference, for example, a copy placed in their file or posted on the wall. Once they are familiar with the steps in the skill they should create their own Graphic Template in their notebooks, rather than fill in a blank photocopy.

The first few times that you teach the skill, model how it is laid out on a chalkboard or chart. You will find that students quickly learn how to lay out the skills and will not need a template in front of them.

- At the top of the page, state the purpose of the description.

Purpose

- Underneath this, list the attributes of each item and the significance for each attribute.

Attribute	**Significance**

- Underneath this, write the name of the item you are describing. Leave enough room so that you can add attributes and details in all directions.

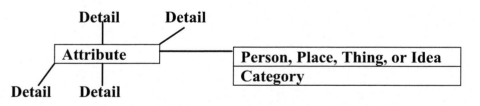

- Once this is complete, write the description.

Description

Students may want to make changes to the information as they articulate their thinking or listen to the ideas of other members of the group. Ensure that you allow them time to modify and refine the information on their Graphic Template.

DESCRIBING

Step One: Close your eyes and try to see the thing that you are describing.

Step Two: Think about the different aspects of the thing that you are going to describe: size, shape, color, texture, smell, sound, etc.

Step Three: Use each of the aspects to describe the object.

Step Four: Read your description to your classmates. Do they know what you are describing?

DESCRIBING

Step One: State the purpose of the description, i.e., humor, explanation, insight, inspiration, or esthetic.

Step Two: Create a mental picture of the item.

Step Three: Verbalize the attributes of each item: size, shape, color, texture, smell, sound, etc.

Step Four: Verbalize how each attribute is significant, using analogies or making connections with prior knowledge.

Step Five: Add details by developing words and phrases that accurately communicate your mental picture to others.

Step Six: Restate or read your description to check for accuracy.

Copyright © Ventures Education Systems Corporation 2003

DESCRIBING

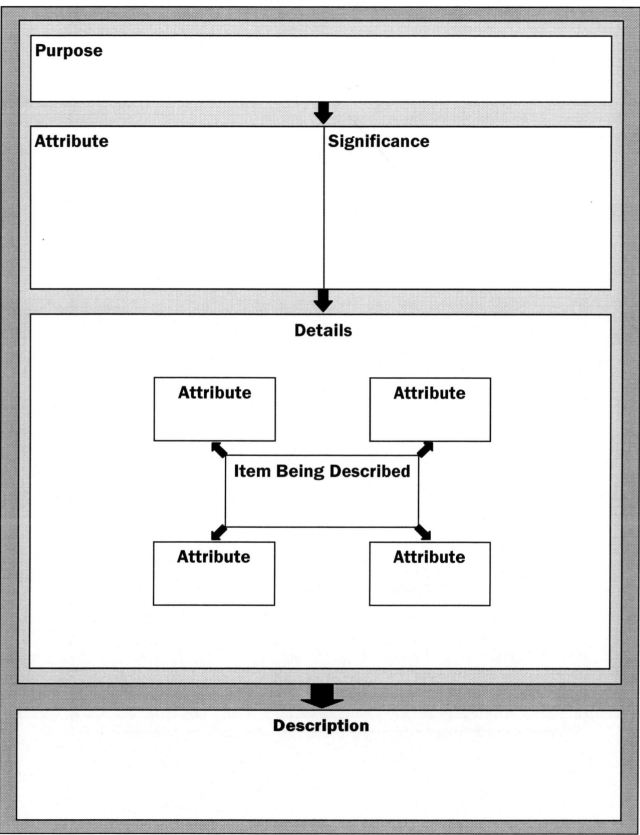

Purpose

Attribute   **Significance**

Details

Attribute   **Attribute**

Item Being Described

Attribute   **Attribute**

Description

Copyright © Ventures Education Systems Corporation 2003

DESCRIBING

Step One: Close your eyes and try to see the thing that you are describing.

Step Two: Think about the different aspects of the thing that you are going to describe: size, shape, color, texture, smell, sound, etc.

Step Three: Use each of the aspects to describe the object.

Step Four: Read your description to your classmates. Do they know what you are describing?

Copyright © Ventures Education Systems Corporation 2003

DESCRIBING

Step One: State the purpose of the description, i.e., humor, explanation, insight, inspiration, or esthetic.

Step Two: Create a mental picture of the item.

Step Three: Verbalize the attributes of each item: size, shape, color, texture, smell, sound, etc.

Step Four: Verbalize how each attribute is significant, using analogies or making connections with prior knowledge.

Step Five: Add details by developing words and phrases that accurately communicate your mental picture to others.

Step Six: Restate or read your description to check for accuracy.

Copyright © Ventures Education Systems Corporation 2003

USING OR CREATING A GRAPHIC TEMPLATE FOR EXAMINING SIMILARITIES AND DIFFERENCES

For directions on teaching Examining Similarities and Differences and ideas for learning activities, reference Chapter 8 in the Ventures In Thinking Teacher Series volume, *Constructive Communication and Structured Thinking in the Classroom, Volume 1.*

Students should have access to the Graphic Template as a reference, for example, a copy placed in their file or posted on the wall. Once they are familiar with the steps in the skill they should create their own Graphic Template in their notebooks, rather than fill in a blank photocopy.

The first few times that you teach the skill, model how it is laid out on a chalkboard or chart. You will find that students quickly learn how to lay out the skills and will not need a template in front of them.

- Identify the two items and list one on the left-hand side of the page and one on the right-hand side of the page.

- Create a table with three columns. Underneath this ask students to list similarities between the two items, the attribute for each similarity, and how it is significant. For example:

Attribute	Similarity	Significance

- Next, create a table with four columns. List all the differences between the two things. Identify the attribute of each difference and explain how each difference is significant.

Attribute	First Item	Second Item	Significance
Color			

- Underneath this, write a summary statement or interpretation.

Students may want to make changes to the information as they articulate their thinking or listen to the ideas of other members of the group.

Ensure that you allow them time to modify and refine the information on their Graphic Template.

EXAMINING SIMILARITIES AND DIFFERENCES

Step One: You are going to examine the similarities and differences between two things. What are they called?

Step Two: Can you say some of the ways that they are alike? When you state a way they are alike, give the attribute. For example, if I say that they are both round, the attribute is shape.

Step Three: Can you say some of the ways that they are different? When you state a difference, give the attribute. For example, if I say that this is blue and this is yellow, the attribute is color.

Step Four: Now look at all of the information. Decide what is important and say a few sentences about the two things that you have compared and contrasted.

EXAMINING SIMILARITIES AND DIFFERENCES

Step One: Identify the two things you are examining.

Step Two: Identify similarities between the two things, the attribute of each similarity, and how each similarity is significant. For example, if I say that they are both round, the attribute is shape.

Step Three: Identify the differences between the two things, the attribute of each difference, and explain how each difference is significant. For example, if I say that this is blue and this is yellow, the attribute is color.

Step Four: Use the similarities, differences, and their significance to state an interpretation or summary regarding the two things.

Copyright © Ventures Education Systems Corporation 2003

EXAMINING SIMILARITIES AND DIFFERENCES

Information

Similarities

Differences

Attribute

Significance

Attribute

Significance

Summary Statement or Interpretation

Copyright © Ventures Education Systems Corporation 2003

EXAMINING SIMILARITIES AND DIFFERENCES

Step One: You are going to examine the similarities and differences between two things. What are they called?

Step Two: Can you say some of the ways that they are alike? When you state a way they are alike, give the attribute. For example, if I say that they are both round, the attribute is shape.

Step Three: Can you say some of the ways that they are different? When you state a difference, give the attribute. For example, if I say that this is blue and this is yellow, the attribute is color.

Step Four: Now look at all of the information. Decide what is important and say a few sentences about the two things that you have compared and contrasted.

Copyright © Ventures Education Systems Corporation 2003

EXAMINING SIMILARITIES AND DIFFERENCES

Step One: Identify the two things you are examining.

Step Two: Identify similarities between the two things, the attribute of each similarity, and how each similarity is significant. For example, if I say that they are both round, the attribute is shape.

Step Three*:* Identify the differences between the two things, the attribute of each difference, and explain how each difference is significant. For example, if I say that this is blue and this is yellow, the attribute is color.

Step Four: Use the similarities, differences, and their significance to state an interpretation or summary regarding the two things.

Copyright © Ventures Education Systems Corporation 2003

EXAMINING SIMILARITIES AND DIFFERENCES

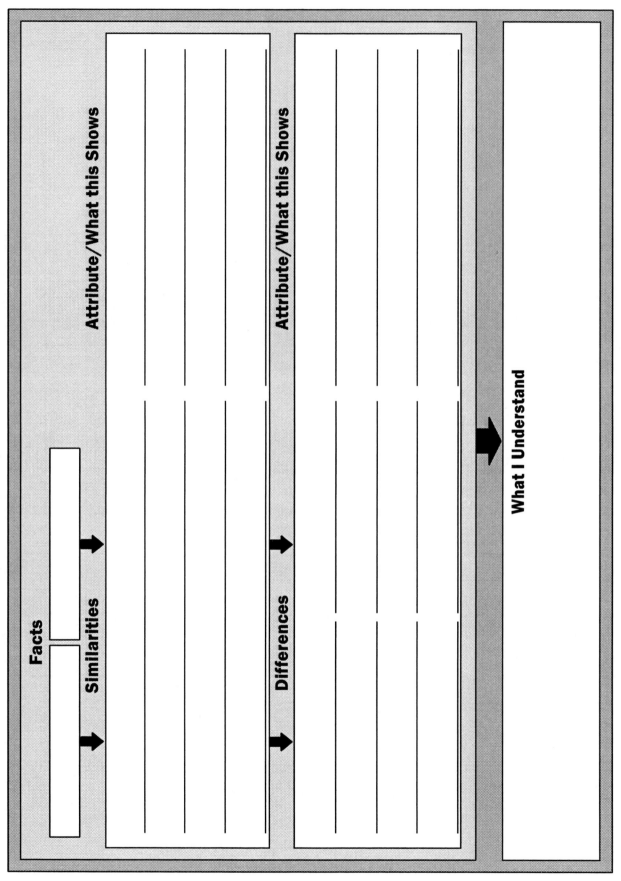

Facts

Similarities

Attribute/What this Shows

Differences

Attribute/What this Shows

What I Understand

Copyright © Ventures Education Systems Corporation 2003

USING OR CREATING A GRAPHIC TEMPLATE FOR ANALYZING THE PARTS OF A WHOLE

For directions on teaching Analyzing the Parts of a Whole and ideas for learning activities, reference Chapter 9 in the Ventures In Thinking Teacher Series volume, *Constructive Communication and Structured Thinking in the Classroom, Volume 1.*

Students should have access to the Graphic Template as a reference, for example, a copy placed in their file or posted on the wall. Once they are familiar with the steps in the skill they should create their own Graphic Template in their notebooks, rather than fill in a blank photocopy.

The first few times that you teach the skill, model how it is laid out on a chalkboard or chart. You will find that students quickly learn how to lay out the skills and will not need a template in front of them.

- State what the whole is at the top of the page. This may be a physical object, a process, a theory, a number of theories, and so on.

The Whole

- Underneath this, ask students to list all the parts of the whole going across or down the page.

- For each part, students identify its function and what would happen if the part were not there.

Part	
If Not There	**Function**

- Students then repeat this process with each part.

- At the bottom of the page, students write a summary statement or interpretation.

Students may want to make changes to the information as they articulate their thinking or listen to the ideas of other members of the group.

Ensure that you allow them time to modify and refine the information on their Graphic Template.

ANALYZING THE PARTS OF A WHOLE

Step One: Name the object.

Step Two: Name the different parts of the object.

Step Three: Choose a part of the object and talk about what the part does and what would happen if that part were not there. Repeat for all the important parts.

Step Four: Say a few sentences about the object and its parts.

ANALYZING THE PARTS OF A WHOLE

Step One: Identify the whole.

Step Two: Identify the parts of the whole.

Step Three: For each part, identify its function and what would happen if that part were not there.

Step Four: Use all the information to state an interpretation or summary to describe how the parts contribute to the whole.

Copyright © Ventures Education Systems Corporation 2003

ANALYZING THE PARTS OF A WHOLE

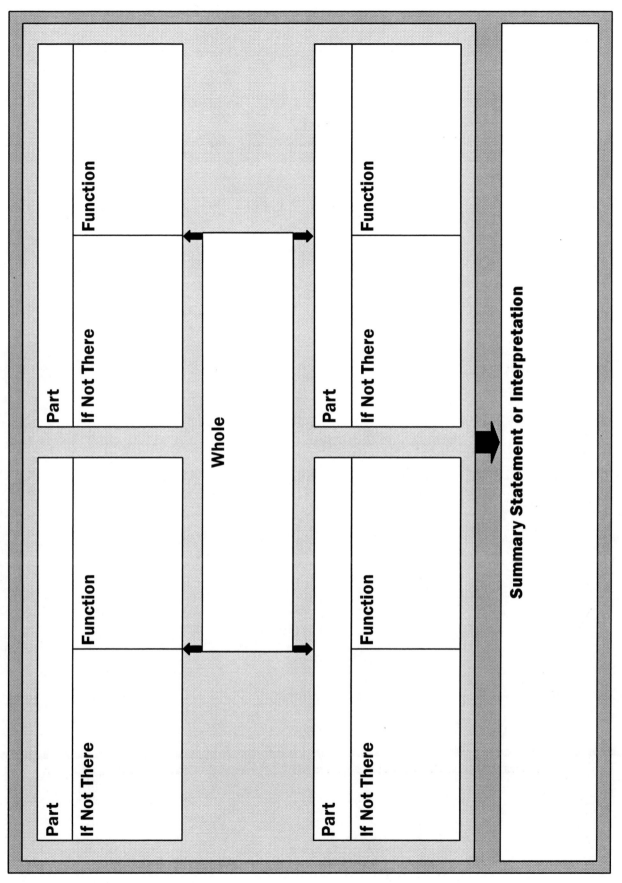

Part | Function | If Not There | Whole | Part | Function | If Not There

Summary Statement or Interpretation

Copyright © Ventures Education Systems Corporation 2003

ANALYZING THE PARTS OF A WHOLE

Step One: Name the object.

Step Two: Name the different parts of the object.

Step Three: Choose a part of the object and talk about what the part does and what would happen if that part were not there. Repeat for all the important parts.

Step Four: Say a few sentences about the object and its parts.

Copyright © Ventures Education Systems Corporation 2003

ANALYZING THE PARTS OF A WHOLE

Step One: Identify the whole.

Step Two: Identify the parts of the whole.

Step Three: For each part, identify its function and what would happen if that part were not there.

Step Four: Use all the information to state an interpretation or summary to describe how the parts contribute to the whole.

Copyright © Ventures Education Systems Corporation 2003

ANALYZING THE PARTS OF A WHOLE

Part			Part			Part		
If Not There	Function		If Not There	Function		If Not There	Function	

Whole

Part			Part		
If Not There	Function		If Not There	Function	

Part			Part			Part		
If Not There	Function		If Not There	Function		If Not There	Function	

Summary Statement or Interpretation

Copyright © Ventures Education Systems Corporation 2003

USING OR CREATING A GRAPHIC TEMPLATE FOR CATEGORIZING

For directions on teaching Categorizing and ideas for learning activities, reference Chapter 10 in the Ventures In Thinking Teacher Series volume, *Constructive Communication and Structured Thinking in the Classroom, Volume 1*.

Students should have access to the Graphic Template as a reference, for example, a copy placed in their file or posted on the wall. Once they are familiar with the steps in the skill they should create their own Graphic Template in their notebooks, rather than fill in a blank photocopy.

The first few times that you teach the skill, model how it is laid out on a chalkboard or chart. You will find that students quickly learn how to lay out the skills and will not need a template in front of them.

There are many examples of graphic templates for both Categorizing and Grouping. Students need to organize the information in a way that is meaningful to them. They may use boxes, a web layout, or a branching diagram. The important thing is that they verbalize their thinking as they are doing the mental processing.

- State what it is that is being sorted.

- Create boxes for each of the categories into which the members are to be placed. You may create a matrix, a branching diagram, a table, or a web.

- Note the key characteristics of each category and then use the matrix, branching diagram, table, or web to place the members

- At the bottom, write a summary statement or interpretation.

Students may want to make changes to the information as they articulate their thinking or listen to the ideas of other members of the group.

Ensure that you allow them time to modify and refine the information on their Graphic Template.

CATEGORIZING

Step One: What are you sorting?

Step Two: What are the categories that you are using to sort the items? What are the characteristics of the category?

Step Three: Place each of the items into the best category and explain why you have chosen that category.

Step Four: In a few sentences, say something about what you did.

CATEGORIZING

Step One: Identify what you are sorting.

Step Two: Identify the categories into which the objects can be placed and the characteristics for each category.

Step Three: Consider each item and describe its characteristics. Place each item and explain why you chose that category.

Step Four: Use all the information to state an interpretation or summary about the items and categories and what you have learned by categorizing in this way.

Copyright © Ventures Education Systems Corporation 2003

CATEGORIZING

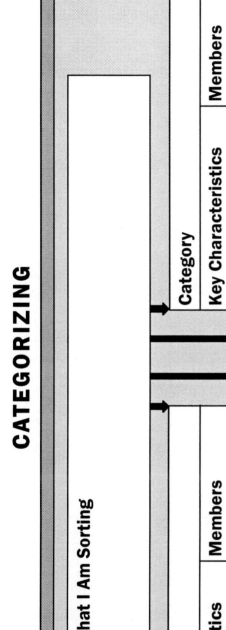

What I Am Sorting

Category

Key Characteristics	Members

Category

Key Characteristics	Members

Category

Key Characteristics	Members

Category

Key Characteristics	Members

Summary Statement or Interpretation

Copyright © Ventures Education Systems Corporation 2003

CATEGORIZING

Step One: What are you sorting?

Step Two: What are the categories that you are using to sort the items? What are the characteristics of the category?

Step Three: Place each of the items into the best category and explain why you have chosen that category.

Step Four: In a few sentences, say something about what you did.

Copyright © Ventures Education Systems Corporation 2003

CATEGORIZING

Step One: Identify what you are sorting.

Step Two: Identify the categories into which the objects can be placed and the characteristics for each category.

Step Three: Consider each item and describe its characteristics. Place each item and explain why you chose that category.

Step Four: Use all the information to state an interpretation or summary about the items and categories and what you have learned by categorizing in this way.

Copyright © Ventures Education Systems Corporation 2003

USING OR CREATING A GRAPHIC TEMPLATE FOR GROUPING

For directions on teaching Grouping and ideas for learning activities, reference Chapter 10 in the Ventures In Thinking Teacher Series volume, *Constructive Communication and Structured Thinking in the Classroom, Volume 1.*

Students should have access to the Graphic Template as a reference, for example, a copy placed in their file or posted on the wall. Once they are familiar with the steps in the skill they should create their own Graphic Template in their notebooks, rather than fill in a blank photocopy.

The first few times that you teach the skill, model how it is laid out on a chalkboard or chart. You will find that students quickly learn how to lay out the skills and will not need a template in front of them.

There are many examples of graphic templates for both Categorizing and Grouping. Students need to organize the information in a way that is meaningful to them. They may use boxes, a web layout, or a branching diagram. The important thing is that they verbalize their thinking as they are doing the mental processing.

- Lay out the objects that you are grouping. Underneath the name, list the characteristics of each object.

Object	Object	Object	Object	Object
Characteristics	Characteristics	Characteristics	Characteristics	Characteristics

- Identify possible categories that you could choose to create groups. Write down the categories.

- Create boxes for each of the categories into which you will group objects. You may create a matrix, a branching diagram, a table, or a web.

- Note the key characteristics of each category and then place the objects.

Every student's Graphic Template may look different. This does not matter as long as each student has gone through the mental steps. Have students show each other what they have done. You can post the responses on the classroom walls. Students will see that there are different forms that they can use and will become skilled at using the one that best suits their need. Remember that it is the mental steps that are important, not the representation.

Students may want to make changes to the information as they articulate their thinking or listen or see to the ideas of other members of the group. Ensure that you allow them time to modify and refine the information on their Graphic Template.

GROUPING

Step One: Look at each item and describe it.

Step Two: Say some ways you could group them. What would your categories be?

Step Three: In a few sentences, say something about what you did.

Step Four: Now Categorize the items.

GROUPING

Step One: Consider each object and describe its characteristics.

Step Two: Identify possible groupings that you could use and explain the significance of grouping this way.

Step Three: State an interpretation or summary about the grouping you are going to use.

Step Four: Group the items using the Structured Thinking Skill of Categorizing.

Copyright © Ventures Education Systems Corporation 2003

GROUPING

Object	Object	Object	Object	Object
Characteristics	Characteristics	Characteristics	Characteristics	Characteristics

Object	Object	Object	Object	Object
Characteristics	Characteristics	Characteristics	Characteristics	Characteristics

Characteristics Chosen To Create Groups

→ **Possible Categories**

Copyright © Ventures Education Systems Corporation 2003

GROUPING

Step One: Look at each item and describe it.

Step Two: Say some ways you could group them. What would your categories be?

Step Three: In a few sentences, say something about what you did.

Step Four: Now Categorize the items.

Copyright © Ventures Education Systems Corporation 2003

GROUPING

Step One: Consider each object and describe its characteristics.

Step Two: Identify possible groupings that you could use and explain the significance of grouping this way.

Step Three: State an interpretation or summary about the grouping you are going to use.

Step Four: Group the items using the Structured Thinking Skill of Categorizing.

Copyright © Ventures Education Systems Corporation 2003

USING OR CREATING A GRAPHIC TEMPLATE FOR ORDERING BY TIME

For directions on teaching Ordering by Time and ideas for learning activities, reference Chapter 11 in the Ventures In Thinking Teacher Series volume, *Constructive Communication and Structured Thinking in the Classroom, Volume 1*.

Students should have access to the Graphic Template as a reference, for example, a copy placed in their file or posted on the wall. Once they are familiar with the steps in the skill they should create their own Graphic Template in their notebooks, rather than fill in a blank photocopy.

The first few times that you teach the skill, model how it is laid out on a chalkboard or chart. You will find that students quickly learn how to lay out the skills and will not need a template in front of them.

- This Graphic Template represents a timeline of some sort.

- At the top of the page identify what is going to be ordered and why.

- In the box underneath identify the purpose and type of ordering.

- Decide whether to use a horizontal or vertical timeline.

- Place dates and times at the appropriate intervals on the timeline.

- Either alongside or underneath, place the events appropriately on the timeline.

- Underneath this, write a summary or interpretation regarding the sequence.

Students may want to make changes to the information as they articulate their thinking or listen to the ideas of other members of the group. Ensure that you allow them time to modify and refine the information on their Graphic Template.

ORDERING BY TIME

Step One: Describe what you are ordering.

Step Two: Place the events in order and explain what you are doing.

Step Three: In a few sentences, say something about when the events happened.

ORDERING BY TIME

Step One: Identify what you are ordering and why.

Step Two: Identify the type of ordering that fits this purpose.

Step Three: Place the events or actions in order according to the interval of time in which they happened or you expect them to happen.

Step Four: Use all the information to state an interpretation or summary regarding the significance of the order.

Copyright © Ventures Education Systems Corporation 2003

ORDERING BY TIME

Purpose of this Ordering

↓

Dates   **Events**

↓

Summary Statement or Interpretation

Copyright © Ventures Education Systems Corporation 2003

ORDERING BY TIME

Step One: Describe what you are ordering.

Step Two: Place the events in order and explain what you are doing.

Step Three: In a few sentences, say something about when the events happened.

Copyright © Ventures Education Systems Corporation 2003

ORDERING BY TIME

Step One: Identify what you are ordering and why.

Step Two: Identify the type of ordering that fits this purpose.

Step Three: Place the events or actions in order according to the interval of time in which they happened or you expect them to happen.

Step Four: Use all the information to state an interpretation or summary regarding the significance of the order.

Copyright © Ventures Education Systems Corporation 2003

ORDERING BY TIME

Purpose of this Ordering

↓

Dates   **Events**

⇩

Summary Statement or Interpretation

Copyright © Ventures Education Systems Corporation 2003

USING OR CREATING A GRAPHIC TEMPLATE FOR ORDERING BY OCCURRENCE

For directions on teaching Ordering by Occurrence and ideas for learning activities, reference Chapter 11 in the Ventures In Thinking Teacher Series volume, *Constructive Communication and Structured Thinking in the Classroom, Volume 1.*

Students should have access to the Graphic Template as a reference, for example, a copy placed in their file or posted on the wall. Once they are familiar with the steps in the skill they should create their own Graphic Template in their notebooks, rather than fill in a blank photocopy.

The first few times that you teach the skill, model how it is laid out on a chalkboard or chart. You will find that students quickly learn how to lay out the skills and will not need a template in front of them.

- At the top of the page identify what is going to be ordered and why.

- Underneath this, identify the purpose and type of ordering.

- Decide whether you need a vertical, horizontal, or cyclical chart. A cycle is good for life cycles or processes that repeat themselves.

- Create boxes for each of the events that you want to record and link them with an arrow.

Either

- Record the events in each of the boxes.

Or

- Split each box in half. In the first section of the box record the event. In the second section record what would happen if the step were missing or incomplete.

- At the bottom, write a summary or interpretation regarding the sequence.

Students may want to make changes to the information as they articulate their thinking or listen to the ideas of other members of the group. Ensure that you allow them time to modify and refine the information on their Graphic Template.

ORDERING BY OCCURRENCE

Step One: Describe what you are ordering.

Step Two: Place the events or actions in order. Talk about the relationship between the steps. What would happen if you skipped a step?

Step Three: In a few sentences, say something about the order of the events.

ORDERING BY OCCURRENCE

Step One: Identify what you are ordering and why.

Step Two: Identify the type of ordering that fits this purpose.

Step Three: Place the events or actions in order and explain the relationship between the steps. Describe what would happen if you omitted a particular step or included one that was incomplete.

Step Four: Use all the information to state an interpretation or summary regarding the significance of the order.

Copyright © Ventures Education Systems Corporation 2003

ORDERING BY OCCURRENCE

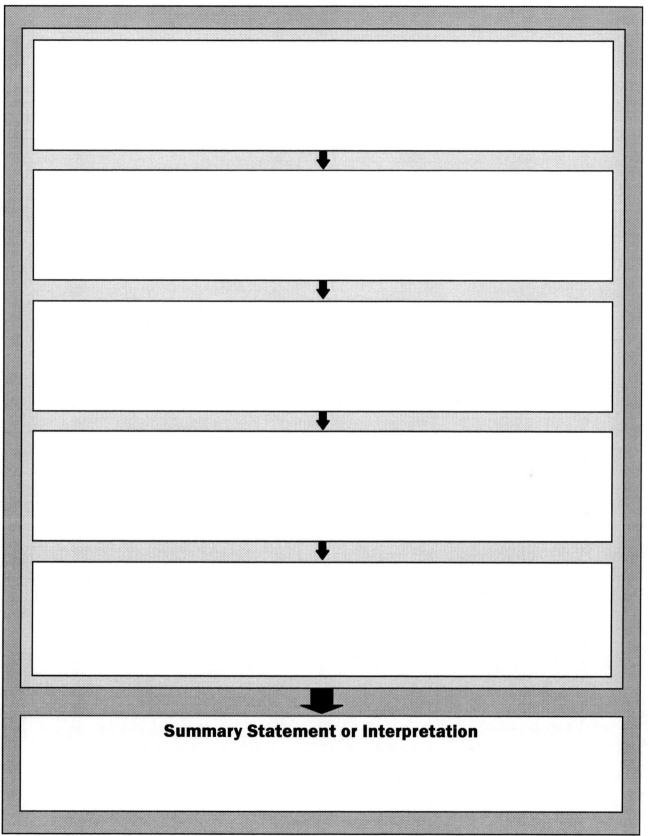

Summary Statement or Interpretation

Copyright © Ventures Education Systems Corporation 2003

ORDERING
BY OCCURRENCE

Step One: Describe what you are ordering.

Step Two: Place the events or actions in order. Talk about the relationship between the steps. What would happen if you skipped a step?

Step Three: In a few sentences, say something about the order of the events.

Copyright © Ventures Education Systems Corporation 2003

ORDERING
BY OCCURRENCE

Step One*:* Identify what you are ordering and why.

Step Two: Identify the type of ordering that fits this purpose.

Step Three*:* Place the events or actions in order and explain the relationship between the steps. Describe what would happen if you omitted a particular step or included one that was incomplete.

Step Four: Use all the information to state an interpretation or summary regarding the significance of the order.

Copyright © Ventures Education Systems Corporation 2003

ORDERING A CYCLE BY OCCURRENCE

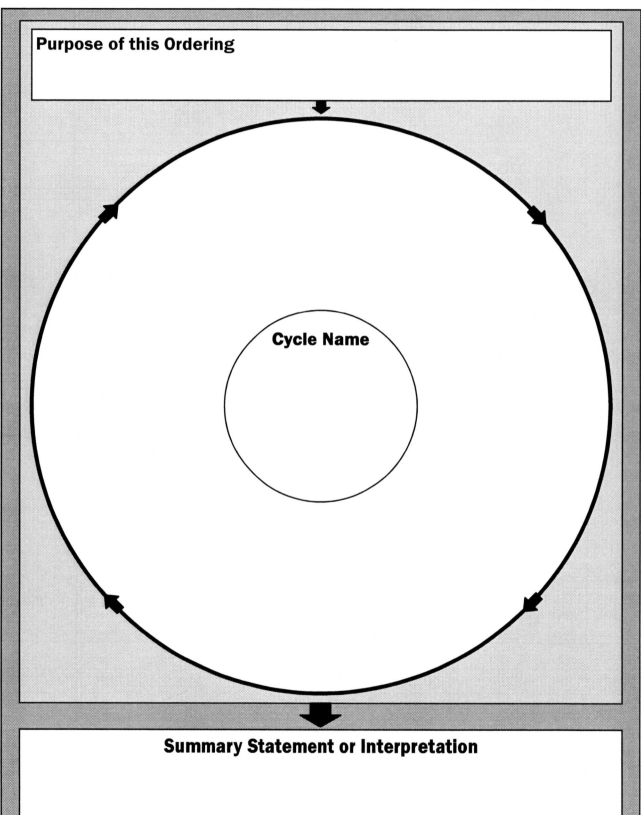

Purpose of this Ordering

Cycle Name

Summary Statement or Interpretation

Copyright © Ventures Education Systems Corporation 2003

USING OR CREATING A GRAPHIC TEMPLATE FOR ORDERING BY RANK

For directions on teaching Ordering by Rank and ideas for learning activities, reference Chapter 11 in the Ventures In Thinking Teacher Series volume, *Constructive Communication and Structured Thinking in the Classroom, Volume 1.*

Students should have access to the Graphic Template as a reference, for example, a copy placed in their file or posted on the wall. Once they are familiar with the steps in the skill they should create their own Graphic Template in their notebooks, rather than fill in a blank photocopy.

The first few times that you teach the skill, model how it is laid out on a chalkboard or chart. You will find that students quickly learn how to lay out the skills and will not need a template in front of them.

- At the top of the page, identify what is going to be ordered and why.

- Underneath this, identify the purpose and type of ordering.

- Below this, identify the criteria that are going to be used for the ordering.

- Then place the information in order, according to how they met the criteria. Next to each item, explain the reason why it has been placed there.

- At the bottom, write a summary statement or interpretation regarding the ordering.

Students may want to make changes to the information as they articulate their thinking or listen to the ideas of other members of the group. Ensure that you allow them time to modify and refine the information on their Graphic Template.

ORDERING BY RANK

Step One: You are going to put these things in order from the_____ to the _____.

Step Two: Place the things in order and give the reasons you ordered them as you did.

Step Three: In a few sentences, say something about the order and the ranking.

- OR -

Step One: Describe what you are placing in order. Say what type of order you are using.

Step Two: Place the things in order and give the reasons why you ordered them this way.

Step Three: In a few sentences, say something about the order and the ranking.

ORDERING BY RANK

Step One: Identify what you are ordering and why.

Step Two: Identify the type of ordering that fits this purpose.

Step Three: Identify the criteria for ranking.

Step Four: Place the items in order according to how they meet the criteria. State the reasons.

Step Five: Use all the information to state an interpretation or summary regarding the significance of the order.

Copyright © Ventures Education Systems Corporation 2003

ORDERING BY RANK

Items Being Ranked

Purpose of this Ranking

Criteria for this Ranking

Item	Reason

Item	Reason

Item	Reason

Item	Reason

Summary Statement or Interpretation

Copyright © Ventures Education Systems Corporation 2003

ORDERING BY RANK

Step One: You are going to put these things in order from the ____ to the ____.

Step Two: Place the things in order and give the reasons you ordered them as you did.

Step Three: In a few sentences, say something about the order and the ranking.

- OR -

Step One: Describe what you are placing in order. Say what type of order you are using.

Step Two: Place the things in order and give the reasons why you ordered them this way.

Step Three: In a few sentences, say something about the order and the ranking.

Copyright © Ventures Education Systems Corporation 2003

ORDERING BY RANK

Step One: Identify what you are ordering and why.

Step Two: Identify the type of ordering that fits this purpose.

Step Three: Identify the criteria for ranking.

Step Four: Place the items in order according to how they meet the criteria. State the reasons.

Step Five: Use all the information to state an interpretation or summary regarding the significance of the order.

Copyright © Ventures Education Systems Corporation 2003

USING OR CREATING A GRAPHIC TEMPLATE FOR SUPPORTING A CONCLUSION

For directions on teaching Supporting a Conclusions and ideas for learning activities, reference Chapter 12 in the Ventures In Thinking Teacher Series volume, *Constructive Communication and Structured Thinking in the Classroom, Volume 1.*

Students should have access to the Graphic Template as a reference, for example, a copy placed in their file or posted on the wall. Once they are familiar with the steps in the skill they should create their own Graphic Template in their notebooks, rather than fill in a blank photocopy.

The first few times that you teach the skill, model how it is laid out on a chalkboard or chart. You will find that students quickly learn how to lay out the skills and will not need a template in front of them.

- Students write the conclusion that they are going to find support for at the top of the page.

- On the left hand side, list any support for the conclusions

- On the right hand side, list any assumptions or unstated reasons

- At the bottom, write a summary statement or interpretation regarding the conclusions and support.

Students may want to make changes to the information as they articulate their thinking or listen to the ideas of other members of the group. Ensure that you allow them time to modify and refine the information on their Graphic Template.

**SUPPORTING A CONCLUSION:
EXAMINING AN AUTHOR'S CONCLUSION**

Step One: What do you think is the author's conclusion?

Step Two: List all the reasons that you can find.

Step Three: What do you think about the author's conclusion?

**SUPPORTING A CONCLUSION:
EXAMINING AN AUTHOR'S CONCLUSION**

Step One: State the author's conclusion.

Step Two: Find and list the support given in the text for this conclusion.

Step Three: Identify any unstated reasons or assumptions the author may be using to support the conclusion.

Step Four: State an interpretation or summary regarding the author's conclusion and support.

Copyright © Ventures Education Systems Corporation 2003

SUPPORTING A CONCLUSION: EXAMINING AN AUTHOR'S CONCLUSION

Author's Conclusion

Reasons

Unstated Reasons or Assumptions

Summary Statement or Interpretation

Copyright © Ventures Education Systems Corporation 2003

SUPPORTING A CONCLUSION: EXAMINING AN AUTHOR'S CONCLUSION

Step One: What do you think is the author's conclusion?

Step Two: List all the reasons that you can find.

Step Three: What do you think about the author's conclusion?

Copyright © Ventures Education Systems Corporation 2003

SUPPORTING A CONCLUSION: EXAMINING AN AUTHOR'S CONCLUSION

Step One: State the author's conclusion.

Step Two: Find and list the support given in the text for this conclusion.

Step Three: Identify any unstated reasons or assumptions the author may be using to support the conclusion.

Step Four: State an interpretation or summary regarding the author's conclusion and support.

Copyright © Ventures Education Systems Corporation 2003

**SUPPORTING A CONCLUSION:
EXAMINING MY OWN CONCLUSION**

Step One: In a few sentences, say something about what you have seen or read.

Step Two: List your support for saying that.

Step Three: Say something about your conclusion.

**SUPPORTING A CONCLUSION:
EXAMINING MY OWN CONCLUSION**

Step One: State a conclusion about what you have seen or read.

Step Two: Find and list the support given in the text for this conclusion.

Step Three: Identify any unstated assumptions related to your support.

Step Four: State an interpretation or summary regarding your conclusion and support.

Copyright © Ventures Education Systems Corporation 2003

SUPPORTING A CONCLUSION: EXAMINING MY OWN CONCLUSION

My Conclusion

Unstated Assumptions

Reasons

Summary Statement or Interpretation

Copyright © Ventures Education Systems Corporation 2003

SUPPORTING A CONCLUSION: EXAMINING MY OWN CONCLUSION

Step One*:* In a few sentences, say something about what you have seen or read.

Step Two: List your support for saying that.

Step Three*:* Say something about your conclusion.

Copyright © Ventures Education Systems Corporation 2003

SUPPORTING A CONCLUSION: EXAMINING MY OWN CONCLUSION

Step One: State a conclusion about what you have seen or read.

Step Two: Find and list the support given in the text for this conclusion.

Step Three: Identify any unstated assumptions related to your support.

Step Four: State an interpretation or summary regarding your conclusion and support.

Copyright © Ventures Education Systems Corporation 2003